I0559030

THE MAGICAL WORLD OF DRAGOR

Kathy Kurk

Contents

Dedication

This book was written for Ryan, with lots of love from mom. Remember always the good old times of us in bed, cuddling and making up, or telling stories. Imagination is a wonderful thing, grow up, but never give up.

Acknowledgment

Thank you first to the bullies of my son, Ryan, in 6th grade. Without you, I would not have written this story. Also, to Ryan, thank you for letting me help you through this rough time, when you thought the world was against you and for letting me tell you a story to help.

Dika Budi N, thank you for working with me and creating the illustrations. You were professional and very helpful to me in my first book. I would like to thank my mom for telling me it was a good story, and I should publish it. It took me years, but I did it, Mom, and I know you didn't think I would be the one in the family to publish a book. I would like to thank my husband for supporting me in all I do and for telling me honestly to do what I feel is right, not what others want me to do.

Thank you, God, for keeping my son safe and in the right mind of space to not harm himself when his class was against him and for opening himself up and letting me help.

Thank you to Logan and Nicholas, the two good friends who helped him through this time as well. You too, Charlotte. Also, Kerry and Jen the mothers who let their sons play and distract and stay friends with him through his hard times. We will always be family, love you guys.

About the Author

Hello, my name is Kathy. I am a mom to a wonderful boy named Ryan, who was bullied in school not once but twice. The first time in 6th grade, when I wrote this story at night to help him sleep and learn that bullies are bullies, but you are the winner, and real friends don't bully. The second time, he was older, and in both instances, the "no tolerance rule" well, I can say in two counties and two different schools, doesn't exist; they did nothing for my son and favored the bullies.

Parents' schools are scared to get sued or whatever, so they do nothing. I will not go into details but know this, I learned something each time that I should do if it happened again, thank God it did not. Also, you are not alone; reach out for help if needed. Bullying doesn't just affect the child, but also the family.

If your child gets bullied, be there for them as a shoulder to cry on and listen to them. It might take time for them to open up, but the night your child says, "Mom, I was wondering if I'd be missed" because of the bullies, hold them tight and do what you can for them. I told him this story, curled up with him each night until he fell asleep and let him know I would miss him and so many more. I held him tight and prayed a lot and I hope that someday there are no bullies. Get them help; if you cannot, let them know they are not alone.

On the second bullying, I finally told the school, well, if they come near my son again, I will not come to you alone, but with the police. It gets bad, bullied or not, hug your children, listen to them when they come to you, and enjoy every moment. I wrote a book

iii

with my son, for my son. If your child is bullied, find something for you two, and like above, take the moments and let them know they are loved and loved forever. Ryan asked for a second book after this one. I did write what he asked. Cherish everything.

If you believe, then you can see the magical world of Dragor. Once you make the long journey you will find many friends to help you along the way. One of those friends is Joseph, the magical blue dragon. He will guide you as you travel to many different worlds and places of Dragor.

Chapter 1
The Beginning

Ryan was a little boy who thought every night that there was a dinosaur under his bed.

This was not a dinosaur, but rather Joseph, the magical blue dragon. He was there to help Ryan jump into a new world where anything can happen.

Our story begins one night as Ryan finds Joseph and realizes he is no dinosaur, and he is very friendly. After a few minutes, Joseph tells Ryan about a magical land far away called Dragor.

Ryan asked, "Where is Dragor?"

Joseph replied, "Dragor is a land you create up in your head. Anything can happen in Dragor."

"Can we go there?" asked Ryan. "Of course, we can, you make it up, so let's go."

So, Ryan jumped onto Joseph's back and off they flew to the land of Dragor.

Chapter 2
Dragor

Joseph said, "Oh, look, we are here," as he landed on some strange little island.

"Joseph, is this where you live?" asked Ryan. "Yes, but while I have friends here, we also must watch out for others who are not so friendly."

"Oh well," said Ryan, "I will be alright. Let me go look around."

"Ok, but please be careful. I heard that Harold the monster snake is on the island, and he is not friendly at all. He likes to scare little boys like you."

"Don't worry, I will look out," said Ryan and off he went into the land of Dragor.

Dragor was a magical land filled with lots of beauty, but Ryan could feel that there was something dark as well.

Chapter 3
Ryan Meets His First Friend, Leo

As Ryan walked along a path, he followed the sound of water. It was like a jungle, trees everywhere. The sun could barely break through the canopy.

Ryan kept walking but he started to hear something, then something touched his shoulder. He stopped suddenly and looked around, but he no longer heard anything, and he could not see anything.

The path started to open a little, and as Ryan came to the end of the trees, he stood there. Something had touched his shoulder again. He turned around as fast as he could and saw nothing. He slowly turned around to see that right in front of him was a beautiful waterfall that fell into a glass clear lake. But then he looked down and there was a little monkey.

Ryan didn't know what to do, so he decided to sit down and get a little closer to the monkey.

Ryan said, "Hello, my name is Ryan, and I am friendly."

The monkey smiled and said, "Hello, my name is Leo. I am sorry if I scared you before, I was trying to find out if you were nice or not."

Ryan and Leo sat there for a while and looked at the waterfall. Leo asked what Ryan was doing. Ryan said, "I am new here and I am going to explore the island of Dragor."

Leo replied right away. "Oh, I could take you around the island. I know it well and can try to keep you away from Harold; he is very mean. He tried to eat me once, but I got away and now I stay far away from him."

Ryan said, "Sure, you can help me explore. Let's get a drink of water and then head out towards those mountains over there."

Chapter 4
The Mountain Region

As Leo and Ryan headed out towards the mountains, the open flats turned into very high grassy lands. Leo jumped up onto Ryan's shoulder. Ryan turned his head and asked Leo what was wrong. Leo said, "I don't like the high grasslands. You cannot see very well here, and you never know what's around you."

Leo started to shake a little, and again Ryan stopped and asked what was up.

Leo said, "Didn't you hear that?" Ryan said, "No, what?" Then they sat still, very still for a minute and they heard a growl. It was close to them. They wondered what it could be, the grass was so thick they could not see. They knew it was not Harold the snake, because snakes hiss.

"Maybe a lion," said Ryan. "That isn't good. We should walk slowly and look carefully until we get out of this thick grass."

8

They walked in a zig zag. Because Ryan felt this way, they might avoid whatever had made that sound. As the grass opened near the bottom of the mountain chain, they felt relief. "We made it out of the grass, and I don't hear anything. Do you, Leo?"

Leo said, "No, I don't hear anything now."

They reached the bottom of the hill and sat under a tree. "We should stay here tonight and climb tomorrow," said Ryan. Ryan built a little hut on the ground, and Leo said, "Oh no, I will stay up in the tree tonight. There are too many critters down on the ground."

As Leo got up to a branch, they heard something coming from the grass. Ryan hid in his hut and looked out the door, and Leo stayed up in the tree. Suddenly, a tiger jumped out of the grass. "Ah ha!" said the tiger. "I found you! I have been tracking you all day, but you kept moving around."

With a shaky voice, Ryan said, "Are you going to eat me?" The tiger said, "Oh no, I was just trying to figure out what the new smell was. I will not eat you. My name is Stripes. Is it ok if I stay the night with you? I can help protect you from others."

"Sure," said Ryan, "but you will not eat my friend Leo either, will you?"

"Who is Leo?" said the tiger! "Leo is my friend, the monkey, look up." Stripes looked up. "No, no, I will not eat your friend Leo. A friend of yours is a friend of mine."

Leo climbed down from the tree and sat right next to Ryan and the tiger. This was the closest either had been to a tiger. Ryan explains that Leo and he were going to explore the island and wanted to climb up the mountain a little to take a better look.

"Oh," said Stripes, "I can help you up the mountain. There are some better ways to go and some hard ones, too. If you don't know where to go, you could end up on the wrong path and get stuck."

"It would be wonderful if you could help us," said Ryan.

"One day on Dragor, and I already have two friends." They all lay down and went to sleep.

10

Chapter 5
The Morning & The Climb

It was a very cold night, and as the sun slowly rose, Ryan, Leo, and Stripes realized they had cuddled together for warmth. "Good morning," they all said. Ryan stood up and stretched out, then he put his hands into his warm pockets.

"Ouch!" Leo jumped, and Stripes asked, "What was the matter?"

Ryan pulled his right hand out of his pocket and said, "Something stung me. Wait, there is something in my pocket." He threw off his jacket and put it on the ground. The jacket slowly moved. Ryan backed up a little and watched as a little hedgehog popped his head out from under his jacket.

The hedgehog stretched his little legs and arms and shook himself. "Sorry, sorry, my name is Brian. I was so cold last night, and I saw you all cuddled up together. I figured you wouldn't mind if little old me cuddled up as well. I found your pocket to be very, very warm. I didn't want to wake you, so I just crawled right in. Hope you don't mind, and sorry I pricked you. I was sleeping, and you startled me."

"No problem," said Ryan, "this is Leo, and this is Stripes, we are traveling around Dragor together."

"Oh, may I come along, too?" asked Brian.

"Sure," they all replied. So, they all warmed up a little, got something to eat, and headed up the mountain.

When they finally reached the top after hours of climbing, Ryan carried Brian and Leo, who rode most of the way on Stripes. They could see the island better now. "Hey, look, there are the swamps, there is the waterfall and the jungle, and over there is the beach."

Leo said right away, "Let's go grab some sun at the beach. Harold the snake doesn't like the beach that much." But off in the distance in the swampy area, there was a light glow.

Ryan wondered what it was. "No," Ryan said, "I would like to head to the swamps."

"The swamps," yelled Leo, "but that is for sure where Harold would hang out."

"Who cares," said Ryan, "I can take care of Harold and I saw something glimmer over that way and would like to see what it is."

12

"Ok," said Stripes, "I will go with you, but we must be cautious. There are lots of creepy things in the swamp."

So, they walked down the mountain and headed toward the swamp. It would take them hours and it would be close to nightfall when they got there. So, they decided they would camp there once they got there and explore in the morning. The journey was hard, as they headed down the mountain, through the high grasses and over to the swamp. They had no idea who or what they might run into, but Ryan was sure of one thing. He saw something glimmering, and it was a sign that he should head that way, or at least that is what he thought.

They reached the edge of the swamp land, and it was starting to get dark, so they found a safe place next to a big old hollowed-out tree.

13

Ryan decided that since this was the swamp and there would be more creatures out at night and mosquitoes, he would start a fire. He had in his bag a fire starter, and his dad had shown him how to use it when they were camping. So, Ryan collected wood and got a fire started. The night would at least be lighter and warmer for the group of friends.

It was a long night with lots of new noises for Ryan. He had not slept well, but he was ready to go.

Chapter 6
The Swamp

Ryan opened his eyes to a marshland filled with all kinds of sounds and green everywhere you looked. They had gotten there so late the night before he really couldn´t see it well.

Ryan, Leo, Brian, and Stripes walked towards the main big body of water to look around. There they saw blueish water surrounded by trees and grassy wetlands. There were many animals as well. They stayed away from the edge of the water, because they had seen a big alligator in the middle.

Across the way was a small island where they spotted three snakes. Right next to them on a small branch of land was a turtle. Life was everywhere you looked. The swamp was alive.

Ryan started to think about what he saw on the mountain top, the glimmer. He tried to picture where it might be and sat down and drew on the ground. He figured out that the glimmer came from Snake Island. Ryan asked the others, "Do you think it would be ok to go over to Snake Island?"

Stripes replied, "Oh, those snakes over there will not hurt you. We just must watch out for Harold."

"Ok."

"So," Ryan then said, "How do we get over there?"

Leo said, "A boat!" "We don't have a boat," said Ryan, "but we could build a raft."

So, the friends worked together and built a raft. They paddled over to Snake Island, and Ryan searched and searched until he found what he had seen. It was gems, a hand full of them.

Ryan collected them wondering how they got so deep into the swamp. As Ryan picked up the last blue gem, he heard a hiss.

"What are you doing?" came from behind a rock. Hiss. "Who are you?" Hiss. Ryan couldn't see anything but could hear it and knew it was a snake. He looked around and the others had already started back toward the raft.

Ryan said, "Hello, come out where I can see you." Ryan remembered that Stripes had said the snakes on that island could not hurt him. But before he remembered the second part, out came a huge snake, a monster snake. He said:" Hiss, my name is Harold."

17

Ryan's face grew with fear. He had never seen a snake this big before. He had heard about Harold, too much about Harold. He didn't want Harold to know how scared he was.

"So," Ryan said, "hello Harold, I am Ryan. I was up on the mountain and saw a glimmer. It called me here where I found these gems. I hope you don't mind."

"Hiss," Harold said, "mind, why would I mind you taking gems? They mean nothing to me." Ryan started to feel better, but just then Harold stood taller and said, "But, hiss, but I do mind people in my space, my area."

18

Ryan could tell Harold was getting madder by the minute, so he said, "Sorry, Mr. Harold, I didn't know this is your space," and started to run faster and faster to the raft. He yelled ahead, "Go, go, get the raft going, Harold is here!" So, Stripes and the others pushed the raft off just as Ryan jumped on.

They all turned to look at Harold slither behind, but luckily for Ryan, he was faster. Harold hissed: "I will find you little boy and I will get you!"

Ryan said, "Let's get out of here," and they all paddled as fast as they could. They knew they needed to get out of the water and swamp fast because once Harold hit the water, he could catch up to them, and that would not be good.

They made it to the other side, jumped off and they all jumped on Stripes, and he ran as fast as he could. They went through the high grasslands and all the way to the beach across the island. They didn't stop once to see if Harold was coming, because Leo and Stripes knew that Harold would be coming. He would hunt them down. Harold always was the king of Dragor, or at least he thought he was.

Chapter 7
The Beach

They had gotten away from Harold for now. Stripes knew he would be ok. But he also knew that Harold would search the whole island for Ryan until he found him.

They walked up and down the beach wondering what they should do. As they walked, they came across a small red crab.

"Hey, hey watch out for us little guys," he said.

20

"Sorry," said Ryan and the others. The crab, known as Reds, noticed they seemed to be in thought and asked. "What was the matter."

Ryan said, "Well, we were in the swamp and ran into Harold, and now he is after me. We are trying to think of somewhere I can go where he will not find me."

"Oh," said Reds, "what about my home, the ocean?" "The ocean, "said Ryan. "Well, I cannot breathe underwater, and I cannot swim for very long either."

"No problem," said Reds and Stripes.

Leo said, "Big problem."

"No, it isn't," said Reds. "Follow me."

"You see, a while back, there was this research team studying the ocean for life. They left in a hurry one day and left this little machine. They used it all the time and they were fine underwater. Follow me, it is right around the corner here."

They wondered what Reds was taking them to. As they turned the corner, they saw it, a little yellow submarine.

"That would work if it worked alright," said Ryan. Leo jumped on board and started to look around. Brian said, "I will come along with you. I am small and will not take up much room."

Stripes said, "Sorry, but I don't like tight places or water. I will stay here on the island. You will be safe in there away from Harold."

Ryan looked at Stripes with sad eyes. He knew this meant goodbye. He ran over, gave Stripes a big hug and said, "Will you be alright here alone?"

Stripes smiled, "Sure, no problem, and I am not alone. I will head back to the jungle and find my family."

"Family," said Ryan. "Oh yes, I have a wonderful family. My wife is due any day now. I was out hunting when I came across you guys. I wanted to help, and it was not a big deal. Now I have a story to tell when I get back."

Ryan hopped aboard the submarine and checked it out. "It looks ok to me." He placed Brian near the steering wheel, right next to a small window. "Leo," he said, "let's see if we can get this thing started."

Broom, broom went the engine. It was running. They climbed to the top, where the hatch was still open, and said goodbye to Stripes and thanked him once again for helping them out. "Ok, Reds, jump on in," said Ryan. Reds said, "No, that is ok, I will be fine and even better out here in the water. I will show you around, you follow me."

So, they closed the hatch and off they went down, down into the sea and Stripes went back to his family.

Chapter 8
The Ocean Blue

As they started to drive, Ryan said, "Let's hope there are no leaks."

Leo made a face and said, "You know, monkeys don't like water either."

"Don't worry, Leo, we will take it slow and test this little guy out."

As they descended under the water, they saw a whole new world. One which they had never seen before. Because Ryan was never under the ocean, and it was for sure that neither was Leo or Brian.

As they came close to the bottom, they all looked out the windows in awe. This was yet another wonderful world and full of life as well. As they looked around, they saw fish, crabs, coral, seaweed, the light from above, and then Leo said, "Oh, look, a starfish. I always wondered what they looked like."

Reds floated in front of the window that Ryan was looking out and said, "Ok, so I just want you to know that this is all beautiful and nice but as it was on the land above, there are also scary, bad things down here. So, we need to watch out. I don't want to be anyone's lunch, you know."

Reds led them around the sea, and they came to a seaweed garden. There was movement in there, and at first, they could not see what it was. They inched a little closer, but not too close, as the seaweed could clog the engine, and they would stall and get stuck there. The seaweed moved some more and out popped a little sea otter. Leo jumped back as he popped out right at his window.

Ryan laughed and said, "Leo, you don't have to be scared, he cannot hurt you in here."

"Hey, where did Reds go?" said Ryan. Then they heard a little bang on the back door. They looked and Reds was yelling, "Let me in, let me in, or I will be lunch." They opened the back hatch. It led to a room that was filled with water. Then, when the hatch closed, it emptied out and they could open the door to the main cabin. Reds felt better. "I will stay here now. It is safer for me. Man, oh man, I could have really been lunch."

25

They all looked out the window and there popped up the little otter again. He was just swimming and playing around. "Otters like to play a lot," said Reds, "but they also like to eat. He will head up to the surface to eat."

They stayed a while and watched how the otter would swim around, play peek-a-boo with them, and finally he caught a clam and went up to the surface to eat.

Chapter 9
The Drop Off

"Let's head over that way a little," said Reds. "We must be careful and go slow. It is the drop off. Here, the ocean opens up a lot, and there is a lot of open blue ocean. Here is where you will find bigger fish."

"Oh," said Brian. "Can we see a shark?"

"A shark, well, yes, I guess you could, but you better hope he is friendly, or we might be in trouble."

"Oh boy," said Ryan, "I would like to see a shark that would be so cool."

So off they went towards the drop-off. As they got closer, they could see that there were fewer and fewer fish.

Reds said, "Well, that is because of the bigger fish and the fishing nets. See, in the open waters, there is room for nets and the big fish to swim. Big fish eat little fish. So, the little fish stay more in the shallows and reefs."

They came to the edge and looked over. They could only see a few feet downwards as it got darker and darker.

"Let's sit here and look at the bottom window," said Brian. "Maybe we can see something."

They all sat around one window and looked down.

Leo said, "Well, that looks really deep."

"Oh, it is," said Reds, "but the caverns are deeper."

"Deeper than that?" said Leo. "Oh yes, and you don't want to fall in the caverns, even bigger animals live there."

As they waited and waited, Leo got bored and fell asleep. Then out of nowhere, a big bump and the others screamed. Leo woke, startled, "What did I miss?" as the others tried looking out the windows, "Do you see it?"

Brian asked. "No," said Reds, "do you see it, Ryan?"

"See what, see what?" said Leo.

28

Then Ryan said, "There it is, come over here." Brian, Reds, and Leo ran over, and right outside the window, a few yards out, swimming was a big old shark.

"Wow!" said Brian, "he is bigger than I thought."

"Yes," said Reds, "and he is still not the biggest thing down here." But before Reds could say anything more, the shark was right up against the glass and said, "Thank you" to Brian.

Brian shook a little as he was a little hedgehog and there was a huge shark. The shark said, "No worries, mate, I will not hurt you. Pretty cool, I always wanted to see a hedgehog."

Brian smiled and said, "Hello." He asked the shark what his name was.

The shark replied, "My name is Max. What is yours?"

"I am Brian. This is Reds, and Ryan." Leo came out from behind Ryan, "and that is Leo."

"Hello," said Max. "I didn't see you there, you know, coming up from the dark and it takes a little to see things better. Sorry if I hurt you."

"You didn't hurt us at all," said Ryan. "We just got startled. We didn't see you coming either and then there you were. We wanted to meet a shark. We have never seen a shark." Then Ryan paused and said, "Well, I mean, I have never seen one in the ocean. I went to the aquarium many times with my mom and dad, and they have sharks there. They are not as big as you, though, Max."

Max smiled, and they talked for a while. They learned all about sharks and Max learned all about them. Neither one knew too much about the other and they had always wondered.

Ryan was surprised to learn that most sharks are nice. "Sure, they need to eat just like the rest of us, but they really don't like humans," Max told Ryan his favorite food was fish.

"I got to get going," said Max. "I only came up to get some dinner, then go back down and wait until I get hungry again."

"Ok," they all said, and thanked Max for spending time with them and talking with them. But before Max left, because they had told him about their story and he knew of Harold, he told them to watch out.

"Watch out for what?" said Ryan. "Well, I heard a rumor that Harold could not find you on the island of Dragor. He figured you must have gotten off somehow and thus called on his friends to help find you."

Ryan said, "Ok, so what does that mean?" Max said, "Well, down here, there is only one friend to Harold if he has a friend at all, and that is the Kraken."

"Kraken," asked Ryan, "what is that?" Reds said, "Oh, Ryan, that is a giant squid. They are very mean, and they can easily take down this little submarine."

Ryan thanked Max for the warning and said that they would try and watch out not to see the Kraken.

Max drifted down into the dark, deep water. Ryan and the others headed away. Reds said, "If we go this way, we will head to the caverns. The Kraken would be there or should be there."

"But," Ryan said, "would he be out looking for us if Harold asked him to find us?"

"Yes," said Reds, "but he is so big that only the reef and shallow would protect you."

"Well, I would like to see the caverns," Ryan said, "this might be the only time I am ever down this deep in the ocean."

Reds said, "Ok, but we must be very careful. The Kraken is sure to sink us if he sees us."

Before they headed out, Ryan decided to talk with the others. "Brian, Leo, come here, I would like to talk to you." So, Ryan gathered them all around and told them he would like to go and see the caverns. He said, "Harold is after me, not you. If you don't want to or you don't feel safe, I can drop you off. I don't want to get you into trouble without you knowing what it is. We all know that Harold means business and that he has spoken with the Kraken. He doesn't know I know. So, I leave it up to you. You decide, and I will then do what you wish."

Brian said right away, "Oh, I am in. What an adventure!" Leo looked like he was about to say something, but then he paused after what Brian had said. Reds said, "I am going. I should be fine. I am small and if Kranky the Kraken does get us, I am hoping I can get out. I can breathe down here; you guys cannot." Leo looked up, then down.

"Are you ok, Leo?" Ryan asked. "Well, it is scary, but I am in. After all, I have been with you since you pretty much landed on Dragor."

So, off the friends went. Everyone had a window and would scream if they saw Kranky. That was their name for the Kraken now.

31

Chapter 10
The Caverns

As they neared the cavern, they didn't see any sign of Kranky, but it was dark. As they passed the opening to the cave, suddenly, they stopped moving.

Brain said, "We are not moving, yet the motor is working. What is going on?" They all looked out the windows forward and then pressed all the way to the window.

Leo looked toward the back. "Oh no! It's Kranky!"

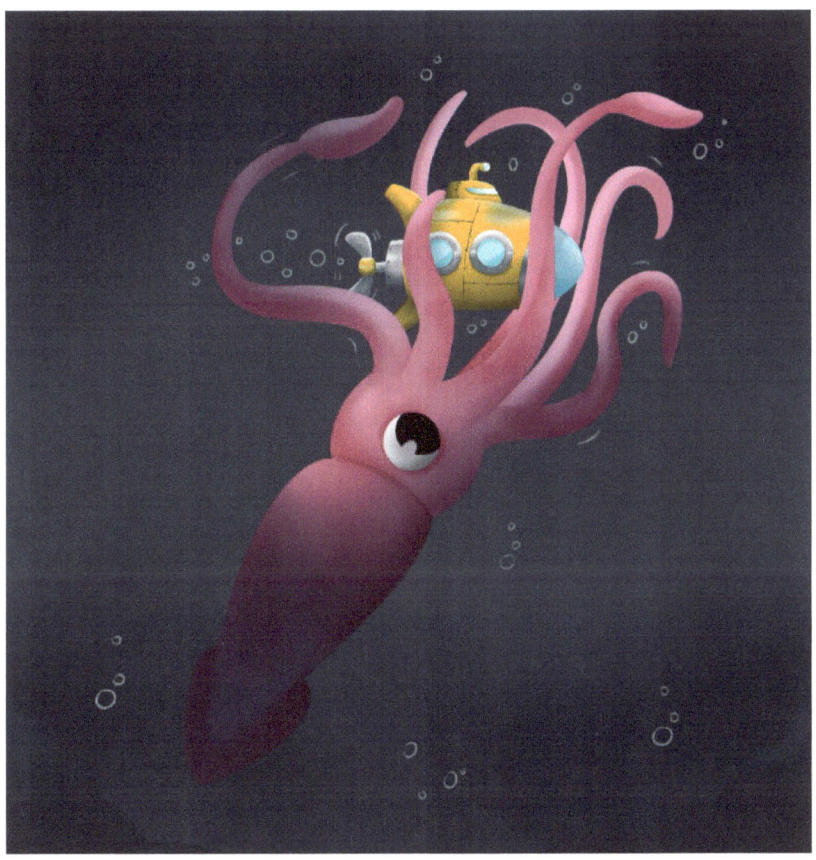

"What are we going to do?" said Brain. Kranky pulled them closer to him and said, "I heard that Harold was looking for you. Now I have you.!" They all looked at each other with dismay in their eyes. Then they heard Kranky say, "Ouch!"

Suddenly, the submarine was free. They started to go away from the cave, but as they turned, they saw that Kranky had been bitten by an otter.

"Hey! It can't be, can it? Is that the same otter who scared us earlier?" Ryan said, "Yes, it is. Let's wait and make sure he is ok."

They watched as the otter stopped and said, "Sorry, but you need to let them go. They are not hurting anyone. Harold is just a big bully who needs to leave them alone." As the two talked, the otter and the Kraken became friendlier.

"Let's get closer," said Ryan.

Leo said, "Are you crazy?" Ryan said, "No, look, they are talking things out and it is friendly, let's go introduce ourselves." So, they headed to the cave again. First, the otter swam by the windows and said hello. Ryan and the others said hello back and "thank you for saving us from Kranky."

"Kranky, who is Kranky?" They all said, "The Kraken, that is our name for him."

The otter said, "You know, he has a real name." Ryan said, "Oh, well this was just our nickname. We didn't really know too much about him except that he was a friend of Harold." Then, the Kraken swam up. Leo stepped back. The Kraken said, "I am not a friend of Harold. Why do you think this?"

"Well, we were told Harold asked you to find us and take us back to him."

"Yes, he did," the Kraken said, "but I was not going to do that. That is what Sprinkles, and I were talking about."

Brian said, "Sprinkles, that is your name!"

"Yes," said the otter, "and this is Inky. He isn't a bad guy, he grabbed you guys and then I bit him because I thought the same. Then he told me he wasn't going to take you to Harold, but he knew a special way through the cave to get you to a rocket on the island."

"Is this true?" Ryan said. "Yes," said Inky. "If you like, I can show you the way." "Thank you, Inky, that would be most helpful. Thank you, Sprinkles, again for saving us from Inky, even if we didn't need it."

So, they all headed deep into the cave. It went left and right and right and left. There were many different paths. There was no way without Inky they would have made it out of the caves.

It was so dark that they had to turn on the lights on the submarine just to see. Sprinkles joined them inside the sub, so he didn't run into any of the walls. Inky was so used to the caves and the dark he was just fine moving around the caves. Then they could see light in the distance. As they got closer, the light came from upwards.

Ryan realized that they had come out of an old volcano that was now a blue hole. "What is a blue hole?" said Brian.

Ryan replied, "A blue hole is an underwater pathway from land, like here, to the ocean. There is a blue hole in the ocean as well as here on land."

"Thank you, Inky."

"No problem," said Inky. "Good luck, the rocket should be right over the hill there. It landed here years ago. The guy on board was picked up by a boat and they left it here."

Ryan and the others opened the hatch and started to climb up the side of the blue hole and over the hill. Sure enough, there was a little rocket sitting right in front of them.

Chapter 11
The Ride Upwards – Space

They all looked at the rocket for the first few minutes, and then Sprinkles said, "Does it work? Can anyone fly it?"

Leo said, "I can."

"What?" said Brian. "Yes, monkeys used to fly into space before humans, and I was one of them. Let's look." The rocket looked good from the outside. Leo climbed inside the rocket and started to check the systems out. Ryan looked to make sure they had enough fuel.

"Ok, looks good," Ryan and Leo said.

Once again, Ryan said to the others, "It could be dangerous; you don't have to come." But without blinking, they all said, "I am in." So, Sprinkles, Ryan, Brian, Reds, and now Captain Leo climbed aboard.

Leo started the procedure and said, "Ok, Brian, you start the count down." The others looked out the windows to make sure things looked good.

Brian started, "Ten, nine, eight, seven." The rocket engine started. "Six."

"Go now!" screamed Sprinkles.

"What is it, Sprinkles?" asked Leo.

"Five," said Brian, as Sprinkles said, "Harold is coming! Lift off now." Leo pushed the takeoff button and off they went up, up into the sky.

As they got higher, the sunlight went into darkness. They had reached space. Ryan looked over as Brian floated to the roof.

"Help, help!" Brian said. Ryan said, "Don't be scared, this is normal in space."

So, as they all settled down and got used to space, they decided to look out the windows and decide where they would head.

"Hey, look over there in the distance," said Leo, "a planet!" So, they all said, "Sure, let's go explore again!"

38

Chapter 12
The Orange Planet

As they landed on this strange little planet, they had to figure out if they could go out and explore. They looked around the rocket and found spacesuits for everyone. There was a ball for Brian, Leo put on a small suit made for kids and so did Ryan.

Reds said, "I will stay here and keep watch on the rocket." Sprinkles found a dog space suit and squeezed in.

They opened the hatch and climbed down the ladder. "Wow, we are on a new planet. We should put a mark that shows we were here."

"Sure, but what?" said Sprinkles. "How about we make a flag?" said Ryan.

"Maybe with a picture of us all on it?"

"Ok, sounds good," said Leo, "but let's go explore."

Before Leo could move, there was something that looked somewhat like a dog right in front of him.

"Don't move," said Ryan, but Leo said, "He looks friendly." So, Leo stuck out his hand and started to pet the creature just as if he was a dog. It got friendlier and friendlier and said, "Who are you?"

"I am Leo, this is Sprinkles, Brian and Ryan." The creature replied: "Hello, my name is Buster."

Buster then said, "We don't get many visitors here."

"We?" said Ryan. "Yes, my friend is just over there at the lake. It was such a nice day, we decided to spend a day at the lake when I heard your rocket. You know good ears and all."

"Come on over and I will introduce you to him." So, Leo, Brian, Sprinkles, and Ryan followed Buster over to the lake, where they saw and met Buster's friend.

"Buster, Buster," he said, "where were you?" Then he saw the others.

"Who are they?" he said.

"Buster," said Pizza, "I would like you to meet Leo, Brian, Ryan, and Sprinkles."

Ryan smiled and said, "Your name is Pizza?"

"Yes, it is!"

"Why?" said Pizza. Ryan proceeded to tell Buster and Pizza what

41

Pizza was.

"Well," he said, "where I am from, we eat pizza." Pizza stepped back and pulled out his laser.

"No!" wait, said Ryan, "we will not eat you. Pizza is a delicious food we eat." He then tried to draw a picture on the ground and Pizza put away his laser.

After talking for a while about Earth, Pizza said, "Ok, it is getting late. Let's go to bed and I can show you around the planet more tomorrow." Pizza took everyone back to his house, and on the way, they stopped and picked up Reds from the rocket so he would not get worried.

Chapter 13
Making New Friends

The next morning, they all awoke and had breakfast.

Pizza said, "Ok, let me go get my ride."

All of a sudden, there was a Pizza with a huge-looking bus. "This is my ride, I built it with parts I found all over the planet. You see people come and just leave their junk. I turn the junk into something like this."

So, they all hopped in and took a ride with Pizza at the wheel. "What is that thing with all the buttons?"

Leo asked. "Oh, well, that controls things like the lights, guns, and radio."

"Guns?" said Brian. "Oh, well, I put them in but so far, I have not needed to use them. We do not get many visitors way out here."

"You saw the lake, now I can take you to the craters. They are fun to surf in. You can take a hover board and spend all day jumping and riding around in the craters. Buster doesn't like that though; he says he gets sick."

After the craters, Pizza said, "Hey, what is that over there, that looks new? It looks like someone is building something." They headed over, but Ryan and the rest were a little uneasy. They didn't know if it would be safe or not.

When they got there, they all looked out the windows to see someone or something had been collecting parts as well and building a small village, and what looked like a rocket. Pizza put the car in park and said, "Be right back, I must check this out. Who else would collect parts and make something out of them?"

The rest waited a few minutes, and then they too went out and looked around.

Buster started to bark, "Ah, I found something!" They all ran over and under a pile of parts, something or someone was hiding. As they all stood around it trying to get a peek at who it might be, the parts flew apart, and out popped a strange-looking object, "Ah! What is it?" Brian said as he hid behind Leo.

Leo said, "I don't know, I have my hands over my eyes. Ryan, what is it?" Ryan took a step closer and looked at this little thing floating in the air.

As Ryan stepped closer, the thing beeped and said, "Hello, I am Glopper." The others jumped back not knowing what this thing was or what it could do. Now everyone, even Pizza, was behind Ryan.

Ryan said, "Hello, I am Ryan," and then introduced the gang.

"What are you?" said Reds.

Glopper replied, "I am an altralink."

"What is an altralink?"

45

"Basically, I am a helper. I lost my person and somehow got here. I got myself rebooted and just started to collect and build to try and find my way back."

"Why the village?" said Pizza. "Well, there are bad storms over here and so it is for protection."

"Oh," Pizza said, "we don't have storms over the other side. You should come with us."

Glopper said, "Ok."

They spent the rest of the day exploring the Planet and Glopper took many pictures. They were all tired from the long day and so they went back once again to Pizza's house.

The next morning, Ryan said, "I think it is time we head back to Dragor." So, Pizza drove them back to the rocket, but when they got there, the rocket would not start. Glopper scanned it and said, "You are out of fuel and your engine is no good."

Reds went into panic mode and screamed: "Oh no, we are stuck here!" Then Pizza said, "You are not stuck here; I have a ship, and I can take you to your Dragor. You have visited and seen my planet, I would like to see yours and maybe try pizza." They all laughed.

Pizza drove to what looked like a hangar for an airplane and opened the doors. There they all saw this strange-looking ship.

"Does that thing fly?" asked Leo.

"Oh yes, and it is very fast too," said Pizza. "Hop in and I will show you around." So, they all hopped in except Glopper. He was outside the door.

Ryan stopped, turned and said, "What is the matter, Glopper, come on?" Glopper got a little brighter, which meant he was happy. He said to Ryan he was not sure he was to come with them.

Ryan said you are always welcome in our group. Glopper flew in and the door closed. Pizza showed everyone around. It was like a royal palace inside. There was a kitchen to eat in, bedrooms, a play area, and so much more.

Then he showed them the control room and said, "Ok. Ryan, you come sit next to me and show me the way to Dragor and I will get you there."

"Deal," said Ryan, and off they went heading back to Dragor.

47

Chapter 14
Back On Dragor

As the rocket landed in an opening near some trees, they heard a loud noise. "Hey, watch where you are parking!" someone yelled. They all looked out the windows to see a little elephant.

"Sorry!" Pizza announced over the loudspeaker to the elephant. "Didn't see you there! One minute and we will come out."

The elephant waited as the door opened and out came all these different creatures. "We are sorry if we scared you, we just came back from a short trip in space and our friend Pizza had to bring us back because our rocket broke." The elephant was still staring at this crowd of mixed creatures.

Ryan walked up and introduced himself. The elephant said, "Well hello," back. "My name is Parker."

They all laughed. "Parker, well, you did a good job parking us." They all smiled and talked for a while.

When Parker heard the story about Harold, he stopped them and said, "Well, Harold was just here. You shouldn't stay here too long."

Then Ryan said, "We will be ok, we have each other and Harold is no match for us."

They decided to keep an eye out but camped there for the night. Then Ryan said it would be time for him to head back home. Leo decided to sleep on top of Parker. He figured he would be safe up there. As they sat around the fire and talked, they heard a growling sound. Brian jumped into Ryan's pocket. Buster did his alien bark and Pizza pulled out his little gun.

The bushes started to open and out popped Stripes. Ryan ran over. "Oh, Stripes, how are you? We missed you!" Brian stuck his head out, "Well, some of us did." They spend the night talking about their adventure and getting to know the new friends. It got late and everyone fell asleep.

The morning came and Leo went out to look for some bananas, but it wasn't long until he came running back to the camp. "Help, help, he is after me." He was on top of Ryan's head, shaking. "Wait, slow down, who is after you?" Just then, through the trees came the familiar hiss. Harold had found them. Buster and Pizza knew of Harold and just stood there with Ryan while the others, even Parker the elephant, stood behind Ryan.

"Well," he hissed, "finally I have you!" Ryan said, "No, you don't!" Harold looked puzzled and said, "What do you mean? I have you!"

Ryan said, "No! You are here, but we are a team, and we are not scared of you. We protect and fight for each other." Harold laughed, gave a big hiss and lunged toward Ryan.

Everyone closed their eyes except Pizza. "Buzz," Pizza shot Harold. "You are a mean bully. Let's cut you down to size and see what you think then."

Everyone heard the buzz and opened their eyes.

Leo said, "Where did he go; did you blast him dead?

"No," said Pizza, "I shrunk him," and opened his hand. "Here he is."

Leo climbed down and took a closer look. "Oh look, such a cutie. Can I keep him, can I?" asked Leo? They all smiled and said, "Sure, but no picking on him." Harold's big hiss was so tiny now they could barely hear it.

Ryan said, "See, friends stick together and help each other when in need. We will always be there for each other."

"Well," Pizza said, "I must get going, come on, Buster, we'd better get home before some other strangers stop by and try to take it." They all stepped way back and waved goodbye. Blast off! Up they went back into the dark skies.

After a few minutes, they heard Joseph flying above looking for Ryan. He landed and Joseph saw all his new friends. "Well, hello to all of you." Joseph knew most of them from the island already.

Leo was playing with something small and laughing a lot. Joseph

51

asked what he had in his hand. When Joseph looked, he saw a small snake. "Harold!" he said, "Is that you?"

"Hiss, hiss, yes, it is me now, put me down." Leo did not put Harold down; he kept Harold as a pet.

"Ok," said Joseph, "time to go, Ryan." Ryan was sad and happy at the same time. He would miss his friends, but he also missed home. Onto Joseph's back, he jumped, and away they flew all the way back to Ryan's bedroom.

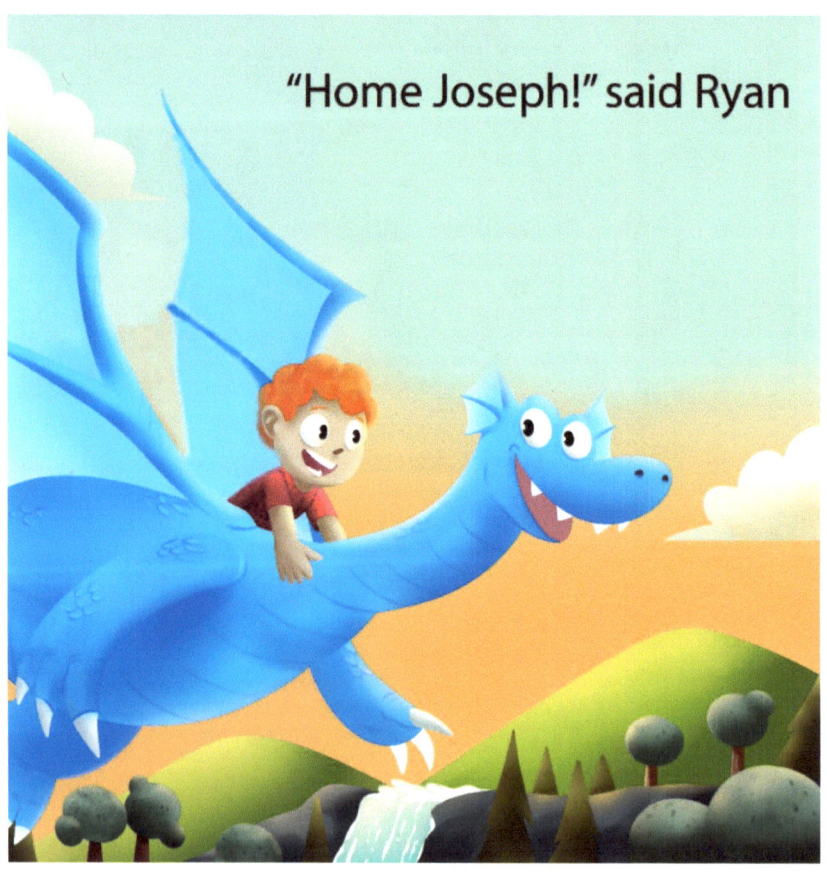

"Home Joseph!" said Ryan

Chapter 15
Ryan Wakes Up

Ryan heard his name softly, then a little louder. He stretched and shook his head. Once he woke up, he realized it was his parents calling him for breakfast. "Time to get up, we have a lot to do."

Ryan remembered his dream. "What a dream!" he thought. Then he put his hand in his pocket and ouch, just like in the dream. In his pocket was a small little hedgehog. "What, how did you get in there?" Ryan was not fully awake.

He ran downstairs with the hedgehog in hand and his parents laughed. "Did you bring that in with you yesterday?" They were so busy and tired from moving to their new home and Ryan had forgotten all about the new home and the move. His eyes lit up and out the door he ran.

You see, what Ryan remembered was that they had moved because his dad had a new job. He bought a zoo. So, when Ryan ran outside, what did he see? Well, a tiger. "Oh boy, he said, "hello Stripes!" He ran around the whole zoo.

To his left was the snake, "Hello, Harold." Then he ran to the aquarium part of the zoo where he saw otters. "Hello Sprinkles, hello Reds, hello Kranky, oh I mean Inky. We know you are not cranky, so we will call you Inky." He went to a big window, and sure enough a shark swam by. "Hello, Max."

He continued around the park, Parker was there. A huge elephant. Then he heard monkeys and ran over to see one with a red cap on. He laughed and said, "Good morning, Leo."

Ryan was happy all his friends were real. He could see them every day. Then he paused a minute and thought to himself: "What about Buster, Pizza, Glopper, and of course Joseph?" Why did he dream about them?

He went back inside, sat down and ate breakfast. After breakfast his dad said, "Ok Ryan, follow me, I finished your room." "My room!" Ryan started up the stairs to his bedroom. "Oh no, Ryan, your playroom, come on down here."

Ryan walked down a winding staircase and then he saw a beautiful room. Painted in a space theme, and there, off in the corner, was an alien, an alien dog, and a little machine that looked like Glopper. His dad turned off the light and all the stars and planets illuminated in the dark. Wow, there was Pizza's planet from his dream. Again, Ryan was happy. Now he had all his friends from his dreams. But, there was still one missing.

Ryan's dad saw his face and asked, "What was the matter?" Ryan told him the whole dream and his dad had a big smile.

"I know who Joseph is," he said, "come with me."

They went outside to the truck. In the back seat, next to where Ryan sat, was a stuffed toy of a blue dragon. Ryan smiled as his dad told him this was his very first toy ever, and he took him everywhere with him. The list was complete. Ryan had a wonderful dream about his old toys, his new playroom, and his new home. Best of all, he knew that they would all be together forever.

Every night, Ryan went to bed happy, and every morning, he woke up happy because he knew that he would always be with his friends. Each night, he had another dream that took him to another land or world, and he made new friends.

Ryan grew up, took over the zoo, and had children of his own, and one day, when they were the right age, he would introduce them to the world of Dragor.

The End